This book belongs to:

_____

Fitness *DAWGS*

COME PLAY WITH THE Fitness DAWGS

By Addie Briggs, MD & Kim Evans, Ed.D.

Illustrated by C. J. Love

"Welcome back to the gym. It is very important that you get some physical activity for 60 minutes each day," Zeus explained.

"I like to play video games," Chill said.

"Video games are fun, but there are other things we can do to move our bodies. Fitness DAWGS, tell Chill what are some of your favorite games or sports you like to play to stay active," Zeus said.

Foo Foo said, "I love football and could play it all day."

"I like all sports that involve running like soccer, lacrosse, basketball, field hockey, and tennis," said Fido.

"But my favorite is track."

Brittany said, "I am happy when I do aerobic exercise like Zumba, spinning, hiking, and swimming."

"Or just dancing."

Boxer said, "I like combat sports like boxing, wrestling, Tae Kwon Do, Muay Thai, Judo, and Mixed Martial Arts."

"I am the best at Tae Kwon Do."

Fee Fee said, "It is always fun when I play basketball with my brother, Foo Foo."

Zeus asked, "Chill, do you have a favorite sport?"

Chill said, "Well, I do like all sports and some of my favorites are baseball, golf, rugby, cricket, and polo."

17

"That's great," said Zeus. "Sounds like you guys like a variety of sports. Do you know any fun games you can play at home to stay active?"

Fee Fee said, "My mom taught us some games she played when she was little like, red light/greenlight, duck duck goose, hopscotch, and double Dutch."

"She taught us how to play musical chairs, too."

Fido said, "My dad taught me how to play kickball, tag, and hide-and-seek."

23

Boxer said, "We can also walk, ride bikes, roller skate, skate board, jump rope or bowl to get in 60 minutes of physical activity each day."

25

Zeus said, "Those are all fun activities to keep you moving. Don't forget to stretch before and after any physical activity. Remember the most important thing is TO HAVE FUN!!!"

List below your favorite activities and sports.

1. _____

2. _____

3. _____

4. _____

5. _____

6. _____

7. _____

8. _____

9. _____

10. _____

Note to parents:

It is recommended that your child participates in 60 minutes of physical activity each day. This is not limited to sports, but also includes your child running around just being a kid. Remember to find an activity that your child likes. The more fun it is, the more likely they will want to participate. Hopefully, this book introduced your child to some new sports like cricket, polo, lacrosse, Muay Tai, and others. You can find out more about these sports by visiting Fitness-DAWGS.com and clicking on Come Play with the Fitness DAWGS. Don't forget "Diet And Workout = Great Success!"

About the Authors:

Addie Briggs, MD and Kim Evans, Ed.D., were each other's first childhood friend. Born six weeks apart, Addie and Kim grew up under the same roof in a duplex. As the youngest children in their families, they spent most of their time playing with each other daily as their older siblings were in school. Around the age of 6, Addie's family moved away and the two best friends lost contact with each other. Forty years later, on August 1, 2015 (which ironically is National Girlfriends Day), Addie spotted Kim in a local restaurant and the two best friends were reunited.

During one of their "catching up" moments, they discovered that they both have a passion for children and have dedicated their lives (Addie as a pediatrician and Kim as a superintendent and lifelong educator) to improving the lives of children. While talking about their passion, they discussed the impact that childhood obesity has on their profession. So, they combined their expertise along with their love for children and created Fitness DAWGS (**D**iet **A**nd **W**orkout = **G**reat **S**uccess). Fitness DAWGS is committed to introducing children to a healthier lifestyle by educating them on good eating habits and physical activity.

Illustrated & Designed By: C.J. Love (Charlie J. Love)
C.love2design@gmail.com
www.clove2design.com

Coming Soon
Book 3 in the FitnessDAWGS series
"Fun At The Farmers Market with the Fitness DAWGS"
FitnessDAWGS.com

Made in the USA
Monee, IL
28 July 2020